A Kalmus Classic Edition

Stephen
HELLER

TWENTY-FOUR PRELUDES
Opus 81

FOR PIANO

K 03515

Kalmus

Twenty-four Preludes.

Ruhig, heiter. (♪ = 144)
Tranquillo, gioioso.

STEPHEN HELLER. Op. 81.

1.

4

Rasch, charakteristisch. (♩ = 138)
Rapido, con espressione caratteristico.

2.

Sehr rasch, etwas im Genre Teniers.
Presto; quasi alla Teniers.

3.

sehr zurückgehalten
molto ritenuto

langsam
lento

8

Bewegt, recitativisch. (♩ = 96.)
Con moto, quasi recitativo.

Nicht schnell, mit wechselndem Ausdruck. (♩ = 112.)
Non allegro, con espressione variata.

Sehr lebendig, reich gefärbt. ($\quad$ = 138.)
Vivacissimo, scintillante.

6.

Mässig schnell; ständchenartig. ($\bullet$ = 116.)
Moderato alla serenata.

7.

Einfach, skizzenartig. (♩ = 138.)
Semplice, quasi bozzetto.

Mit rascher Leichtigkeit hingeworfen, in der Art einer Federzeichnung.
Thrown off swiftly and easily, like a pen-and-ink sketch.

Lebhaft, mit prägnantem Rhythmus. (♩.= 100.)
Vivace, con ritmo pregnante.

11.

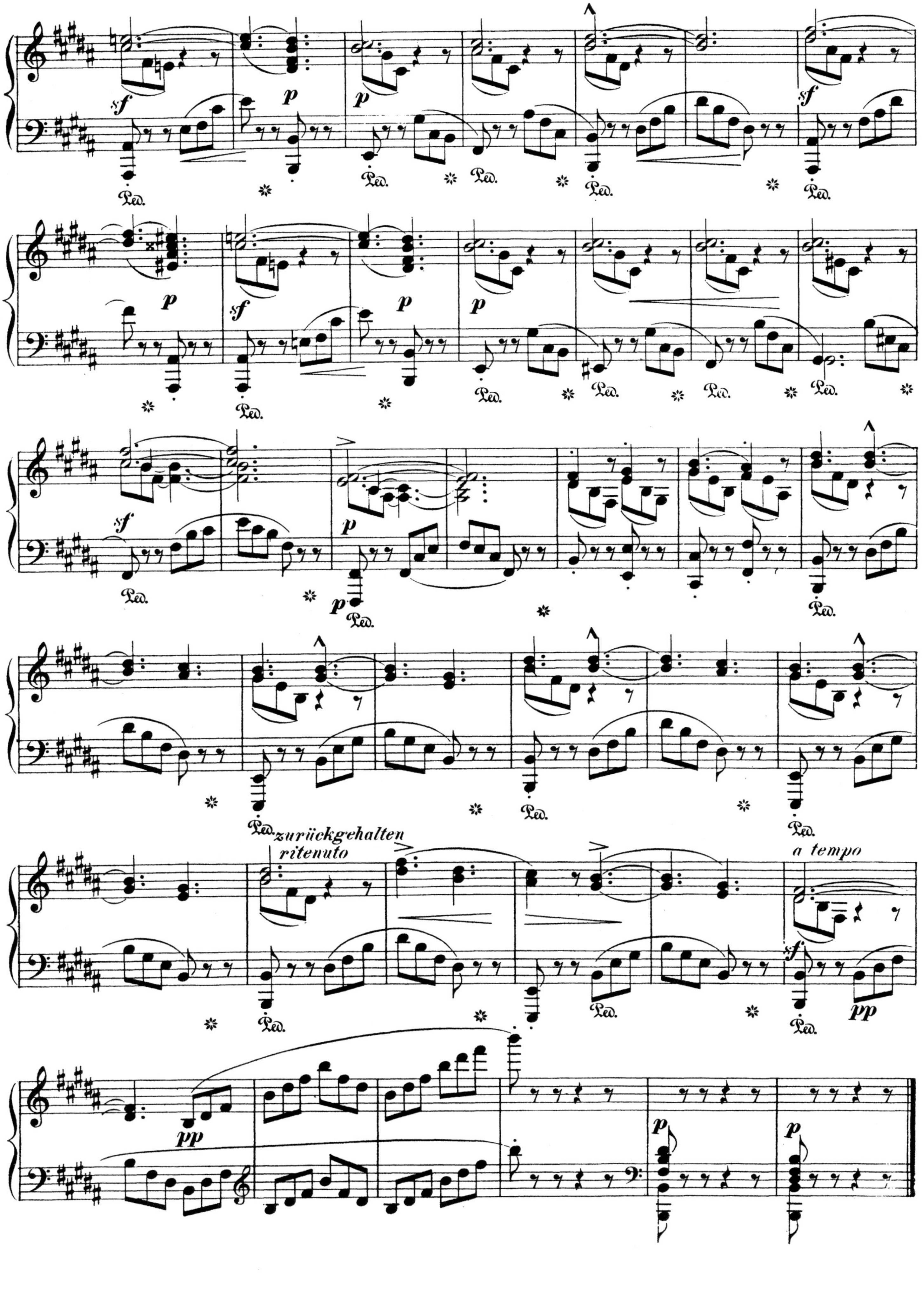
zurückgehalten
ritenuto
a tempo

Leidenschaftlich. (♩ = 122.)
Appassionato.

14.

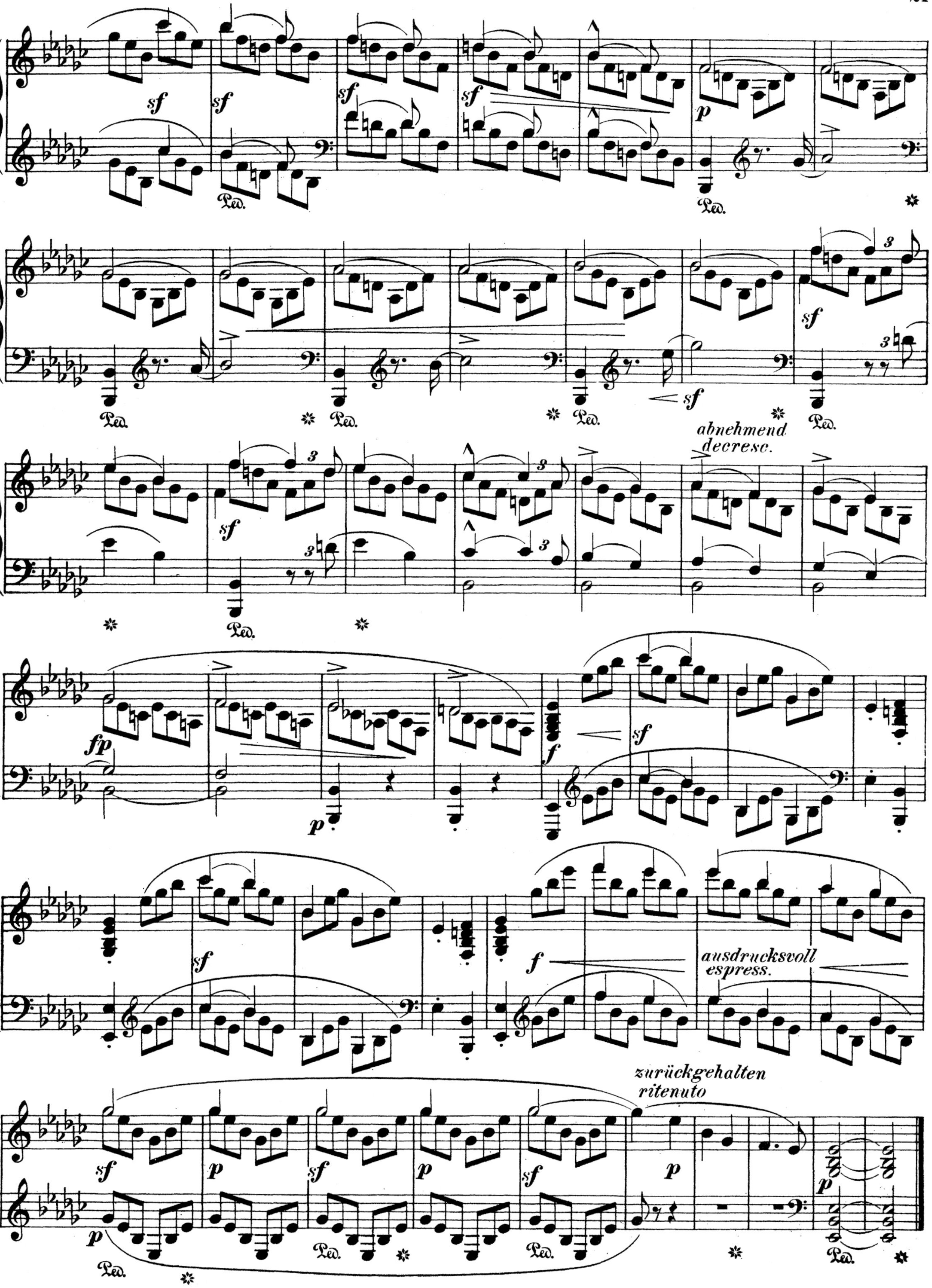
abnehmend
decresc.
ausdrucksvoll
espress.
zurückgehalten
ritenuto

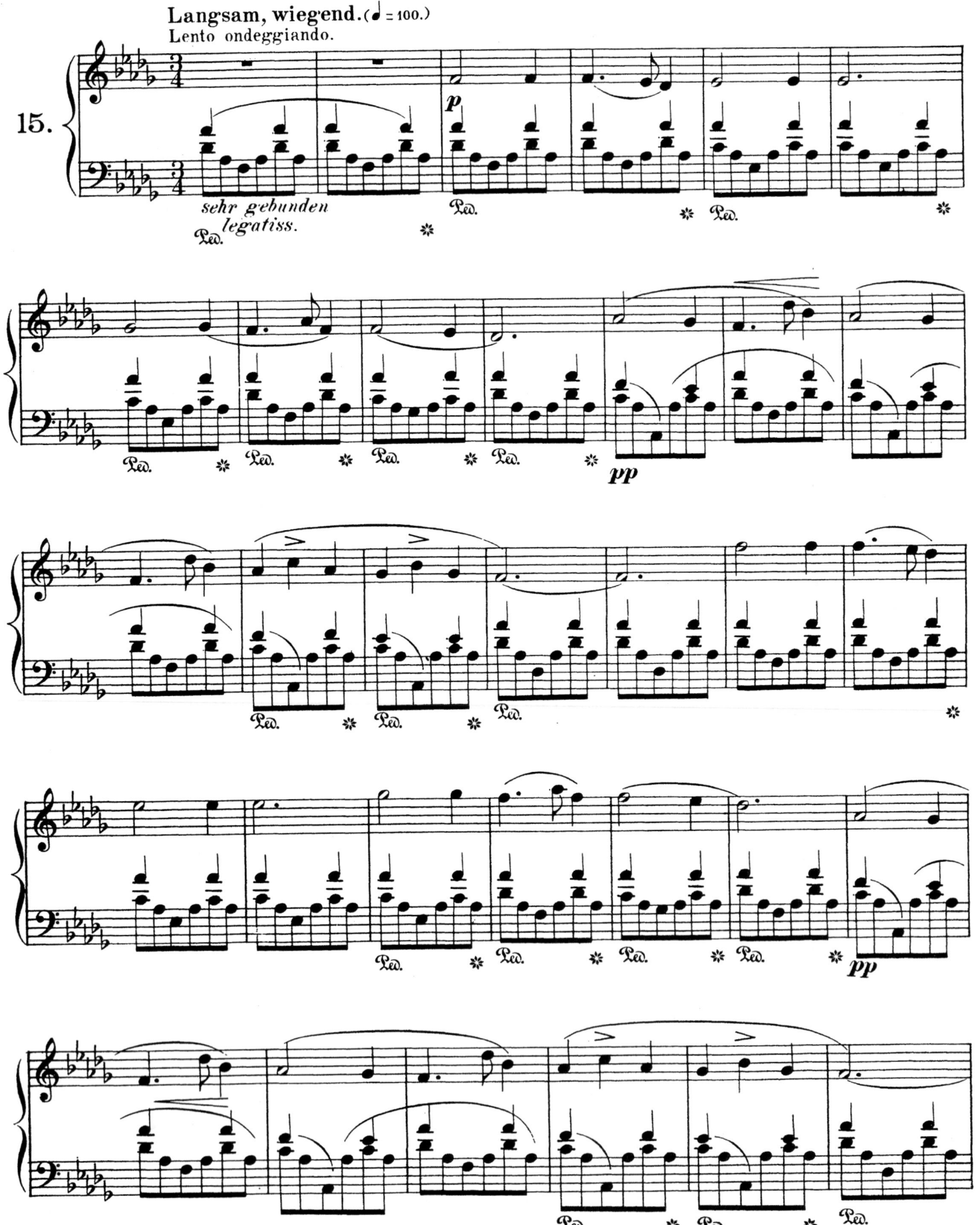

Sehr langsam; ernst, schwermüthig. (♩ = 84.)
Molto lento; serioso, malinconico.

16.

Heiter gesungen. (♩·=72)
Gioioso, cantando.

17.

Keck, energisch. (♩ = 152.)
Fiero, energico.

18.

_f_

_f_ _dröhnend_
tonando

_ff_

_sf_

sff _sf_ _sf_ _sf_ _sf_ _sf_ _f_

_ff_

_ff_ _sf_

_sf_

sff _sf_ _sf_ _sf_ _sf_ _sf_

_sf_ _sf_

Mit leichter Grazie. (♩=152.)
Leggero con grazia.

19.

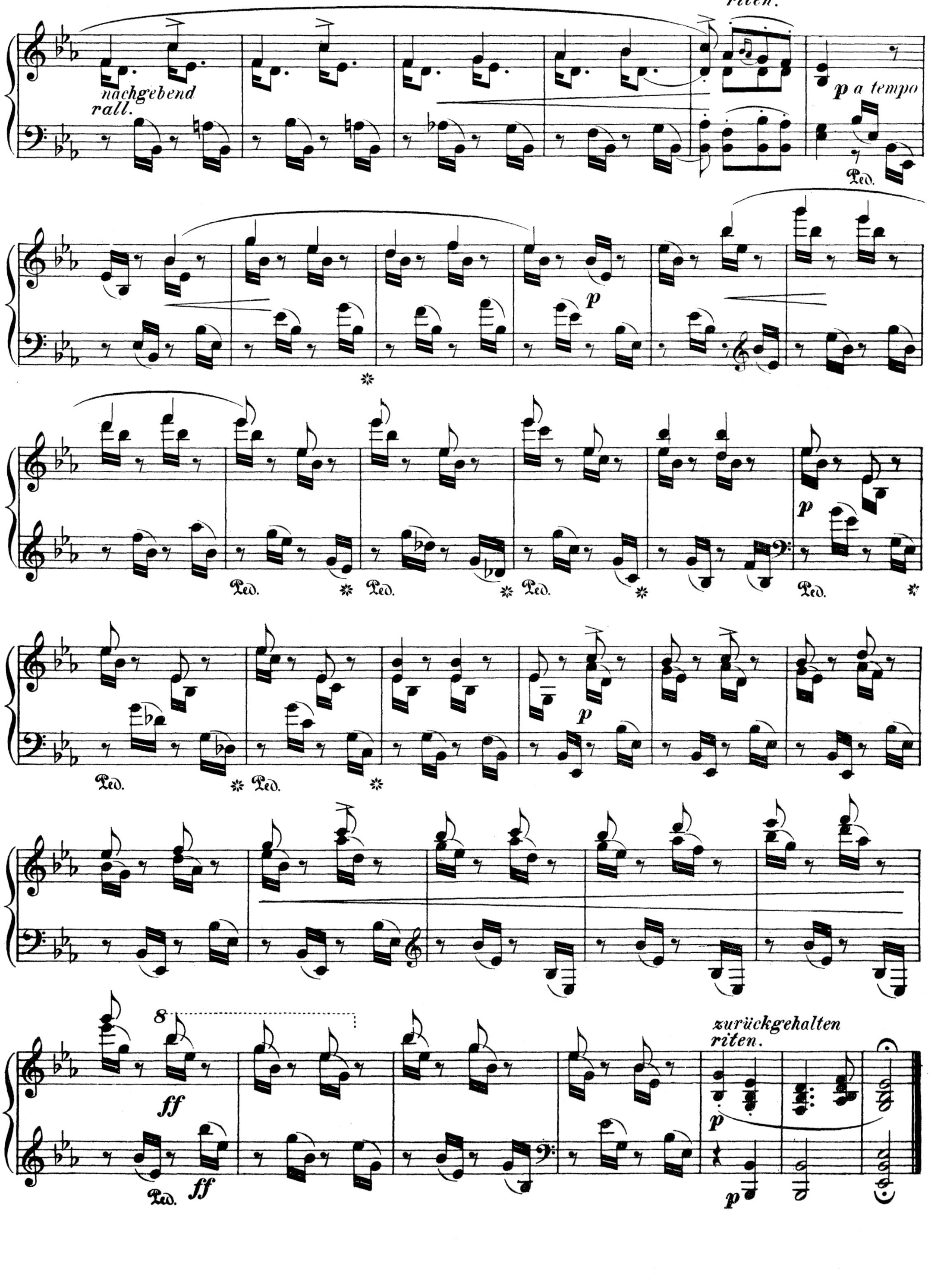
riten.
nachgebend
rall.
p a tempo
Ped.
p
8
ff
zurückgehalten
riten.

Sehr langsam. (♩. = 46)
Molto lento.
Mit dem Ausdruck bittern Schmerzes. (con espressione di dolore amaro)

Zart, aber lebhaft. (♩=84)
Delicato ma vivace.

21.

Lebendig, charakteristisch vorzutragen. (♩. = 126.)
Vivace con espressione caratteristico.

22.

Heiter, unbesorgt.($\text{♩.} = 72.$)
Gioioso, negligente.

23.